T0137603

# A Morning
## with my three
# months old

## Lorry C Francois

AuthorHouse™
1663 Liberty Drive
Bloomington, IN 47403
www.authorhouse.com
Phone: 833-262-8899

Because of the dynamic nature of the Internet, any web addresses or links contained in this book may have changed
since publication and may no longer be valid. The views expressed in this work are solely those of the author and do
not necessarily reflect the views of the publisher, and the publisher hereby disclaims any responsibility for them.

Any people depicted in stock imagery provided by Getty Images are models,
and such images are being used for illustrative purposes only.
Certain stock imagery © Getty Images.

This book is printed on acid-free paper.

ISBN: 978-1-6655-0929-9 (sc)
ISBN: 978-1-6655-0928-2 (e)

Library of Congress Control Number: 2020923630

Print information available on the last page.

Published by AuthorHouse  11/30/2020

authorHOUSE®

# A Morning with my three months old

By Lorry C Francois

"A Morning with my
three months old"

He starts giving me
the wake up mode

I start kissing him

He smiles and giggles

I pick him up

He makes the googling sound
I kiss him again, and hold him closer
I see happy feet (the baby's feet)
I say "I love you"

He (baby talk) googoogaga

I think he's saying

"well mom,

I do love you too,

you know"

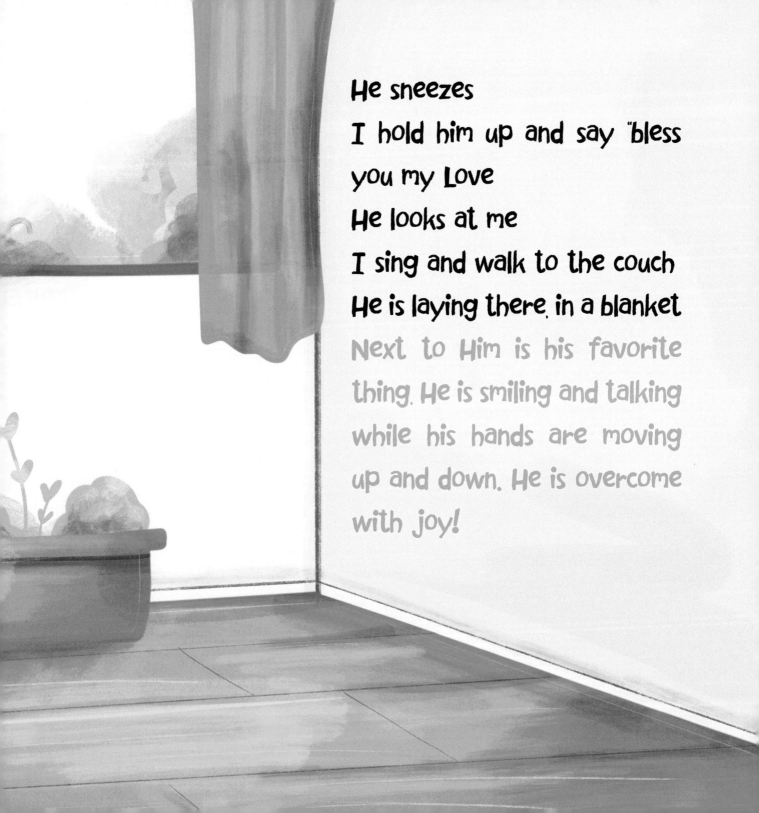

He sneezes
I hold him up and say "bless you my Love
He looks at me
I sing and walk to the couch
He is laying there in a blanket
Next to Him is his favorite thing. He is smiling and talking while his hands are moving up and down. He is overcome with joy!

In the kitchen she makes food

He is playing with the chacha

I walk to the couch

He is moving with excitement

I pick him up

I feed him while I sing " .mon dou dou.
je t'aime de tout mon coeur.

tu sais que manmie t'aime beaucoup mon
doudou. A chaque fois que je

te regarde. je t'aime beaucoup plus maintenant q'avant..

Oui Oui Oui mon boubou ouuuuuuuu"

(My sweetheart, I love you with all my
heart, you know mommy love you

from here past the moon. every time
I look at you. I love you more

than before yeah yeah yeah my love)

He smiles

I say

"I'm happy I love you!"

# About the Author

As a mother and a member of a big family, Lorry C Francois has experienced her shares of stories and adventures. She uses these adventures in her book and her writings. A genuine experience of a mother's daily joy and struggles raising a child guided by these stories shared.

Lorry C Francois was raised in Haiti and emigrated to the United States at an early age. She put herself to school, got into modeling and acting and took time to travel and learn different cultures. The lessons learned growing in a big family environment inspired her to share her own story with the world. Her stories are filled with love, learning, happiness, sadness and most importantly discovering herself through the eyes of a child.

Lorry currently resides in New York with her son and her partner.

# Describe your time and moments with your little one.

_____

_____

_____

_____

## A morning with you?

_____

_____

_____

_____

# How you make me feel?

_____

_____

_____

_____

# Joy of having you!

_____

_____

_____

_____

# Loving moment/s:

_____

_____

_____

_____

_____

Love always, Mom.

_____

_____

_____

_____

_____

Printed in the United States
By Bookmasters